Douglas DC-6

Boeing 707

Shorts 330

Guide to Airport Airplanes

William and Frank Berk

Yakovlev Yak-42

Aérospatiale/British Aerospace Concorde

Douglas DC-3

Boeing 767

McDonnell Douglas DC-10

Lockheed C-130

Plymouth Press

Plymouth Press, Ltd.

42500 Five Mile Rd.
Plymouth, MI 48170-2544
U.S.A.

The authors especially wish to thank the following individuals and organizations: Thomas R. Cole, Boeing Aircraft; Harry Gann, McDonnell Douglas Aircraft; Ray Scippa, Continental Airlines; Rick Varney and Cindy O'Hara, Burlington International Airport; Dick James, Imagepro; Keith Brown, Brown/Dickson Associates.

All silhouettes copyright © Greenborough Associates, Ltd.

The back cover photographs of Shorts 330 (top) and Boeing 747-200F models (bottom) are courtesy of Snort Brothers and Boeing Aircraft, respectively.

The following photographs are courtesy of the National Air and Space Museum, Smithsonian Institution: page 11, photo # 92-13712; page 61, U.S. Air Force Foreign Technology Division photo # 92-13708; page 79, U.S. Navy photo # 92-13703; page 99, U.S. Coast Guard photo # 92-13711.

Printed in the U.S.A.

Contents

Typical modern airliner

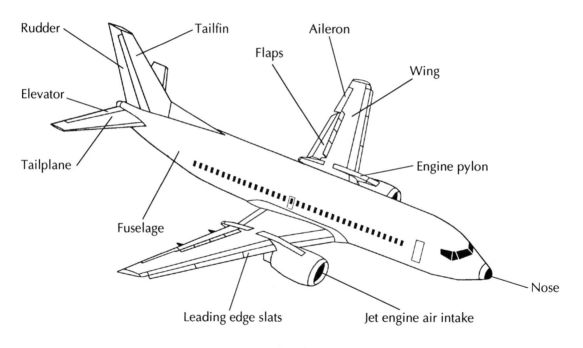

Rudder

Tailfin

Aileron

Flaps

Wing

Elevator

Tailplane

Engine pylon

Fuselage

Leading edge slats

Jet engine air intake

Nose

Introduction

The intent of the *Guide* is to facilitate rapid identification by amateur observers of commonly observed airport airplanes. Virtually all airplanes flown by major airlines are included in the *Guide*.

Although the *Guide* may be browsed, it is designed to be used as follows:

1) Turn to page **vi** to find the group to which the unknown plane belongs. Groups are based on engine number, type, and location on each plane, and the point at which wings are attached to each plane's fuselage.

2) Turn to the page number indicated. This is the first page for each group.

3) Follow the directions to find the subgroup to which the unknown plane belongs.

4) Use the distinguishing characteristics listed under the "Look-alike" section for each plane to tell it from other planes in its subgroup. Note that the "Look-alike" section is not intended to be used to distinguish individual planes from all others in the *Guide*.

To identify a plane, begin here:

If the plane is large with a delta wing, which is swept back and in the shape of an isosceles triangle, with 2 of the 3 sides the same length, and looks generally like this:

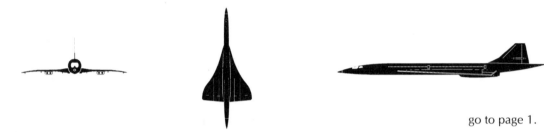

go to page 1.

If the plane has 4 jet engines, 2 on each wing, and looks generally like this:

or has 6 jet engines, 3 on each wing, and looks generally like this:

go to page 5.

If the plane has 2 jet engines, 1 on each wing, and looks generally like this:

or has 3 jet engines, 1 on each wing, with the third on the tail, and looks generally like this:

go to page 23.

If the plane has 2, 3, or 4 jet engines, all of which are on the tail, and looks generally like this:

or this:

or this:

go to page 41.

If the plane has 4 propeller engines, 2 on each wing, and wings which extend from low on the fuselage, and looks generally like this:

or has wings which extend from high on the fuselage, and looks generally like this:

go to page 67.

If the plane has 2 propeller engines, 1 on each wing, and wings which extend from low on the fuselage, and looks generally like this:

go to page 85.

If the plane has 2 propeller engines, 1 on each wing, and wings which extend from high on the fuselage, and looks generally like this:

go to page 113.

Jet airplane with a large delta wing

If the plane is a large transport with a delta wing which is swept back and in the shape of an isosceles triangle—with two of the three sides the same length—it must be the **Aérospatiale/British Aerospace Concorde**, go to page 2.

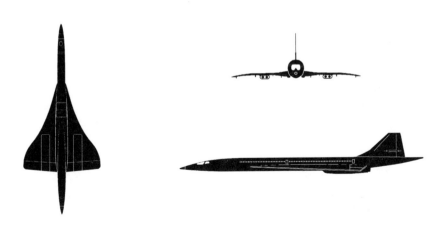

Aérospatiale/British Aerospace Concorde

Nations: France/United Kingdom

First flown: 1969

Length: 205.7ft (62.1m)   **Wingspan:** 83.8ft (25.6m)

Passenger capacity: 128-144

Cruising speed: 1354mi (2166km)/hr at altitude of 51,300ft

Range: 4090mi (6544km)

Look-alikes: Concorde is the only large delta wing aircraft in commercial service. A Soviet supersonic passenger transport, *Tupolev Tu-144,* was externally similar, but is no longer in service.

The product of an Anglo-French collaboration, planning for the Concorde began in 1962. The first prototype flight was made in 1969 with commercial service initiated in 1976. Concorde is the world's only commercial supersonic transport, capable of travel at Mach 2 for 3900 miles. For its makers, however, the plane has not been profitable—only 18 were produced and Concorde is flown only by British Airways and Air France.

Photo courtesy Air France

Jet airplanes with 4 or 6 jet engines, all on wings

If the plane looks generally like this, with 2 jet engines on each wing, and wings extending from low on the fuselage, go to pages 6 to 13.

Boeing 707.....p. 6
Boeing 747.....p. 8
Ilyushin IL-86.....p. 10
McDonnell Douglas DC-8.....p. 12

If the plane looks generally like this, with 2 jet engines on each wing, and wings extending from high on the fuselage, go to pages 14 to 19.

Antonov An-124.....p. 14
British Aerospace 146.....p. 16
Lockheed C-5 Galaxy.....p. 18

If the plane looks generally like this, with 3 jet engines on each wing, it is the **Antonov An-225**, go to page 20.

Boeing 707

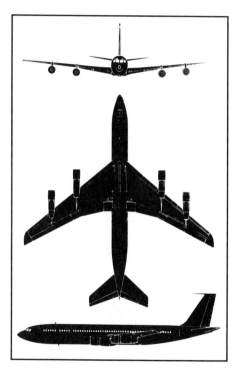

Nation: United States

Versions: 707-120; 707-320 and 707-420 (stretched fuselage and improved engines); 720 (short range); EC-135 (electronic countermeasure); KC-135 (military tanker)

First flown: 1954

Length: 152.8ft (46.6m)   **Wingspan:** 145.6ft (44.4m)

Passenger capacity: 150-189

Cruising speed: 605mi (968km)/hr

Range: 4300mi (6880km)

Look-alikes: Boeing 707 is very similar to *McDonnell Douglas DC-8,* but is different in having a slightly differently shaped tailfin and in usually having an antenna pointing forward from the top of the tailfin. *Boeing 747* has a distinctive hump on the top of the front of its fuselage. *Ilyushin IL-86* is a wide bodied plane, flown only by Aeroflot, the airline of the former Soviet Union.

Originally conceived and developed as a mid-air military refuelling tanker (KC-135), the civilian Boeing 707 was the first American built jetliner. Commercially it was also the most successful of the first generation of long distance jets. In addition to the tanker, military versions include the electronics countermeasure EC-135, which has a large radar dome atop the fuselage. A variant was employed for American presidential transport as Air Force One until supplanted by a specially designed Boeing 747. *Specs:* 707-320; *Silhouette:* 707-320; *Photo:* 707-320.

Photo courtesy Boeing

Boeing 747

Nation: United States

Versions: 747-100, 747-200 (improved engines, longer range), 747-200C (passenger/cargo), 747-200F (cargo), 747SR (550 passengers, short range), 747 SP (shortened fuselage, range 9625 miles), 747-300 (upper fuselage extended aft to accommodate 37 additional passengers), 747-400 (long-range version with extended wings and winglets which extend upward from the ends of the wings)

First flown: 1969

Length: 231.9 ft (70.7m)   **Wingspan:** 195.4 ft (59.6m)

Passenger capacity: 516

Freight capacity: 264,438 lb (120,199kg)

Cruising speed: 602mi (963km)/hr

Range: 7595mi (12,150km)

Look-alikes: The distinctive hump in the forward area of the fuselage housing the pilot's cabin and first class compartment distinguishes Boeing 747 from all other very large jet planes.

Originally conceived in 1965, the Boeing 747 was the world's first jumbo jet; it remains the largest commercial passenger transport, with many versions and continued evolution. The current production model, designated 747-400, has a range of 8406 miles (13,450 km). Special models are used to transport the U.S. space shuttle in "piggy-back" fashion and the U.S. president in Air Force One. *Specs:* 747-200; *Silhouette:* 747-400; *Photo:* 747-400.

Photo courtesy Boeing

Ilyushin IL-86

Nation: Russia

First flown: 1976

Passenger capacity: 350-375

Length: 195.2ft (59.5m)   **Wingspan:** 157.8ft (48.1m)

Cruising speed: 590mi (944km)/hr

Range: 2858mi (4572km)

Look-alikes: *Boeing 707* and *McDonnell Douglas DC-8* are narrow bodied, while IL-86 is wide bodied and is flown only by Aeroflot, the airline of the republics of the former Soviet Union. *Boeing 747* has a distinctive hump on the top of the front of its fuselage.

The IL-86 is the first Soviet wide bodied airliner. Test-flown in 1972, it did not enter service until 1980. Aeroflot is the only airline flying this plane.

Photo courtesy Smithsonian Institution

McDonnell Douglas DC-8

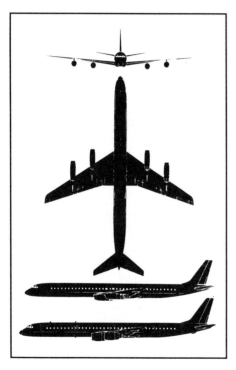

Nation: United States

First flown: 1958

Versions: Series 10, Series 20 through 70 (stretched fuselages, improved engines, freight versions)

Passenger capacity: 173-259

Length: 187.3ft (57.1m)   **Wingspan:** 148.3ft (45.2m)

Cruising speed: 554mi (887km)/hr

Range: 4500-7700mi (7200-12320km)

Look-alikes: *Boeing 707* is very similar to DC-8, but is different in having a differently shaped tailfin and in usually having an antenna pointing forward from the top of the tailfin. *Boeing 747* has a distinctive hump on the top of the front of its fuselage. *Ilyushin IL-86* is a wide bodied plane, flown only by Aeroflot, the airline of the republics of the former Soviet Union.

With the Boeing 707 and the British Comet, the DC-8 pioneered the jet age in the late 1950's. Production of the many versions of this successful airplane continued into the 1980's. About 70 are still in service. *Specs:* Series 60; *Silhouette:* Series 63; *Lower side view silhouette:* Series 73; *Photo:* Series 10.

Photo courtesy Harry Gann/McDonnell Douglas

Antonov An-124

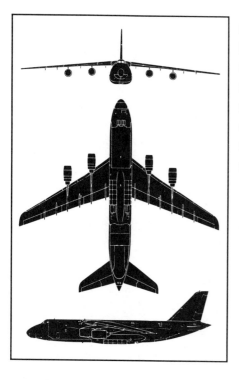

Nation: Ukraine

First flown: 1982

Length: 226.6ft (69.1m)   **Wingspan:** 240.4ft (73.3m)

Passenger capacity: 80 on upper deck

Freight cap: 336,353lb (152,196kg) on lower deck

Cruising speed: 537mi (859km)/hr

Range: 10,252mi (16,403km)

Look-alikes: *Lockheed C-5* has tailplanes which extend from the the top of tailfin, while An-124's extend from the bottom. An-124, although similar in form to *British Aerospace 146,* is three times as long.

The An-124 was the largest plane in the world until the introduction of the An-225. Unlike the U.S. military equivalent very large transport jet, the C-5, the An-124 is used for civilian as well as military purposes. About 20 were in use in 1989 with production set at 10 per year.

British Aerospace 146

Nation: United Kingdom

Versions: Series 100, Series 200 and 300 (stretched fuselages), BAe 146-QC Convertible (passenger or freight), BAe 146-QT Quiet Trader (freight)

First flown: 1981

Length: 93.8ft (28.6m)   **Wingspan:** 86.3ft (26.3m)

Passenger capacity: 82-128

Cruising speed: 477mi (763km)/hr

Range: 1708mi (2733km)

Look-alikes: British Aerospace 146's relatively small size and four jet configuration distinguish it from all other much larger airliners and transports with four jets on their wings.

A short-haul jet, this airplane has a distinctive profile with its four jets and wings attached to the body high on the fuselage. It is in use in North and South America, Europe, Asia, and Africa. *Specs:* Series 100; *Main silhouette:* Series 200; *Lower side view silhouette:* Series 100; *Photo:* Series 200.

Photo courtesy British Aerospace

Lockheed C-5 Galaxy

Nation: United States

Versions: C-5A, C-5B (improved wings)

First flown: 1968

Length: 247.7ft (75.5m)   **Wingspan:** 222.8ft (67.9m)

Passenger capacity: 345

Freight capacity: 265,640 lb (120,199kg)

Cruising speed: 571mi (914km)/hr

Range: 7595 mi (12,152 km)

Look-alikes: *Antonov An-124* has tailplanes which extend from the bottom of the tailfin, while C-5's extend from the top. C-5, although similar in form to *British Aerospace 146,* is three times as long.

The C-5 won out against a version of the Boeing 747 as a large capacity transport for the U.S. Air Force. It was the largest plane in the world until the Soviet Union produced the An-124 (1982) and An-225 (1988). An upward-hinged nose allows straight in loading via a ramp.

Photo courtesy U.S. Air Force

Antonov An-225

Nation: Ukraine

First flown: 1988

Length: 275.5ft (84.0m)   **Wingspan:** 290.0ft (88.4m)

Passenger capacity: 70 on upper deck

Freight capacity: 551,155lb (250,000kg) on lower deck

Cruising speed: 528mi (845km)/hr

Range: 2796mi (4475km)

Look-alikes: An-225 is the only large transport with six jet engines, three on each wing.

Derived from the An-124, the An-225 is the world's largest airplane. In comparison to the single tailfin of the An-124, its twin tailfins facilitate piggyback transport atop the fuselage of large loads, such as the Soviet Union's space shuttle, much in the manner the Boeing 747 is used by NASA to transport the U.S. space shuttle. Despite its mammoth size, its interior cabin dimensions are similar to those of the An-124.

Photo Link photo

Jet airplanes with 2 jet engines on wings

If the plane looks generally like this, with 2 jet engines, both on the wings, go to pages 24 to 35.

If the plane looks generally like this, with 2 jet engines on the wings, and a third jet engine mounted on the tail, go to pages 36 to 39.

Airbus A300

Nations: France, Germany, Spain, United Kingdom
Versions: A300, A300-600 (increased range), A300-600R
  (greatest range)
First flown: 1972
Length: 177.4ft (54.1m)   **Wingspan:** 147.3ft (44.9m)
Passenger capacity: 247-375
Cruising speed: 567mi (907km)/hr
Range: 5075mi (8120km)
Look-alikes: A300 differs from *Airbus A310* in having a longer
  fuselage, but similar wingspan. A300 has a nose which tapers
  to a slimmer point and a fuselage which extends further behind
  the tailfin than both *Boeing 767*, which is also wide bodied,
  and *Boeing 757*, which is narrow bodied. *Airbus A320* and
  Boeing 737 are much smaller, narrow bodied aircraft.

The A300 was the first transport built by Airbus, the aircraft company co-founded by aviation concerns in four European countries, and intended to challenge U.S. domination by Boeing and McDonnell Douglas of the commercial jet market. *Specs:* A300-600; *Silhouette:* A300; *Photo:* A300-600.

Photo courtesy Continental Airlines

Airbus A310

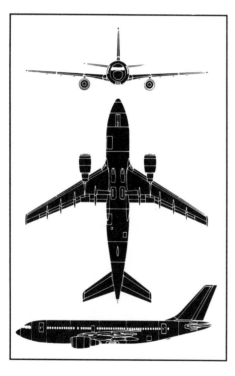

Nations: France, Germany, Spain, United Kingdom

Versions: A310-200, A310-200C (convertible airliner-freighter), A310-200F (freighter), A310-300

First flown: 1983

Length: 153.2ft (46.0m)   **Wingspan:** 144.0ft (43.9m)

Passenger capacity: 200-280

Cruising speed: 518mi (829km)/hr

Range: 5700mi (9120km)

Look-alikes: A310 is a shorter fuselage version of *Airbus A300,* with similar wingspan. In comparison to *Boeing 757* and *767,* A310 has a nose which tapers to a sharper point and a fuselage which extends further behind the tailfin. *Boeing 757* is also narrow bodied in contrast to wide bodied A310. *Boeing 737* and *Airbus 320* are narrow bodied and much smaller than A310.

A shorter fuselage and lower capacity version of the A300 with an improved wing, this airliner has as its main competitor the Boeing 767, to which it is very similar in appearance. *Specs:* A310-200; *Silhouette:* A310-200; *Photo:* A310-300.

Airbus A320

Nations: France, Germany, Spain, United Kingdom

Versions: A320-100, A320-200 (greater fuel capacity and range)

First flown: 1987

Length: 123.0ft (37.5m)   **Wingspan:** 111.2ft (33.9m)

Passenger capacity: 150-179

Cruising speed: 526mi (842km)/hr

Range: 3,305mi (5288km)

Look-alikes: Narrow bodied A320 is much shorter than wide bodied *Airbus A300, Airbus A310,* and *Boeing 767,* as well as narrow bodied *Boeing 757.* The fuselage of A320 extends further behind the tailfin than on *Boeing 737, 757,* and *767.*

The first commercial aircraft, other than the Concorde, to employ "fly-by-wire" control as opposed to conventional hydraulic systems, the A320 is the smallest offering in the Airbus series.

Photo courtesy Airbus Industrie

Boeing 737

Nation: United States

Versions: 737-100, 737-200, 737-300, and 737-400 (stretched fuselages), 737-500 (long range)

First flown: 1967

Length: 109.6ft (33.4m)   **Wingspan:** 94.8ft (28.9m)

Passenger capacity: 115-170

Cruising speed: 576mi (968km)/hr

Range: 1870-3430mi (2992-5448km)

Look-alikes: Narrow bodied Boeing 737 contrasts with wide bodied and much larger *Airbus A300* and *A310,* and wide bodied *Boeing 767. Boeing 757* is wide bodied and 30% longer than Boeing 737. The tail of *Airbus A320* extends further behind the tailfin than on Boeing 737.

With over 2000 produced, the Boeing 737 is the world's best selling commercial jetliner, and of Boeing's current offerings, the smallest. Although the -500 variant has a range of 3040 miles, the 737 was designed as a short-haul aircraft. The current 737-300 through -500 versions are the latest in a continuing evolution which began in 1967. *Specs:* 737-300; *Silhouette:* 737-300; *Photo:* 737-400.

Photo courtesy Boeing

Boeing 757

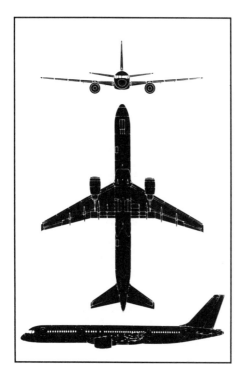

Nation: United States

Versions: 757-200, 757-200PF (freighter), 757-200M (mixed passenger, cargo)

First flown: 1982

Length: 155.1ft (47.3m)   **Wingspan:** 125.0ft (38.1m)

Passenger capacity: 178-239

Cruising speed: 531mi (850km)/hr

Range: 5297mi (8475km)

Look-alikes: In comparison to *Boeing 767*, Boeing 757 is narrow bodied. *Airbus A300* and *A310* are wide bodied and have noses which taper to sharper points and fuselages which extend further behind the tailfin than on narrow bodied Boeing 757. Boeing 757 is almost 30% longer than *Airbus A320* and *Boeing 737*.

The Boeing 757 was originally conceived as an evolutionary narrow bodied follow-up to the Boeing 727, but emerged as an almost completely new design, with wing mounted engines, in contrast to the tail mounted engines of the 727. The similarity of the 757's flight deck to that of the Boeing 767 allows pilots to qualify to fly both airliners concurrently. *Specs:* 757-200; *Silhouette:* 757-200; *Photo:* 757-200.

Photo courtesy Boeing

Boeing 767

Nation: United States

Versions: 767-200, 767-200ER (increased range), 767-300 (stretched fuselage), 767-300ER (maximum range)

First flown: 1981

Length: 159.0ft (48.5m)   **Wingspan:** 156.1ft (47.6m)

Passenger capacity: 216-255

Cruising speed: 531mi (850km)/hr

Range: 4433mi (7093km)

Look-alikes: Boeing 767 is wide bodied, whereas *Boeing 757* is narrow bodied. *Airbus A300* and *A310* have noses which taper to a slimmer points and fuselages which extend further behind the tailfin than on Boeing 767. In comparison to *Airbus A320* and *Boeing 737*, Boeing 767 is wide bodied and almost 50% longer.

A medium range high capacity wide bodied aircraft very similar in appearance to and in direct competition with the Airbus A310. *Specs:* 767-200; *Silhouette:* 767-200; *Photo:* 767-300.

Photo courtesy Boeing

Lockheed Tristar L-1011

Nation: United States

Versions: 1011-1, 1011-100, 1011-200, 1011-250, 1011-500 (improved engines and in the case of the -500, a shortened fuselage to achieve longer range)

First flown: 1970

Length: 177.8ft (54.2m)   **Wingspan:** 155.1ft (47.3m)

Passenger capacity: 246-400

Cruising speed: 567mi (907km)/hr

Range: 4065mi (6504km)

Look-alikes: Tristar L-1011 is different from *McDonnell Douglas DC-10/MD-11* in having its tail engine exhaust located below the engine's air intake on the rear of the fuselage instead of directly behind the intake as in *DC-10/MD-11*.

S imilar in performance and layout to the DC-10, its more successful competitor, the L-1011 was Lockheed's last effort to build a commercial jet transport. In addition to extensive use by airlines, the L-1011 has been adapted to tanker service by the Royal Air Force (U.K.). *Specs:* 1011-1; *Silhouette:* 1011-500; *Photo:* 1011-500.

Photo courtesy Lockheed Aircraft

McDonnell Douglas DC-10/MD-11

Nation: United States

Versions: DC-10 Series 10, 30, 40 (30 and 40 have longer wings); MD-11 (stretched fuselage)

First flown: (DC-10) 1970; (MD-11) 1986

Length: 182.0ft (55.5m)   **Wingspan:** 165.3ft (50.4m)

Passenger capacity: 255-405

Cruising speed: 567mi (907km)/hr

Range: 4633-5788mi (7413-9620km)

Look-alikes: DC-10 differs from *Lockheed L-1011* in having its tail engine exhaust located directly behind the engine's air intake, whereas in *DC-10* the tail engine exhaust is located slightly below the engine's air intake on the rear of the fuselage.

The DC-10/MD-11 are intermediate range jumbo jets which are very similar to Lockheed's Tristar. The U.S. Air Force tanker version is designated KC-10. *Specs:* DC-10-30; *Silhouette:* MD-11; *Photo:* DC-10-30.

Photo courtesy Harry Gann/McDonnell Douglas

Jet airplanes with 2, 3, or 4 jet engines, all on tail

If the plane looks generally like this, with just 2 jet engines, 1 on each side of the rear fuselage, go to pages 42 to 55.

If the plane looks generally like this, with 3 jet engines, 1 on each side of the rear fuselage, and a third mounted on the tailfin, go to pages 56 to 61.

If the plane looks generally like this, with paired jet engines attached to each side of the rear fuselage, go to pages 62 to 65.

Aérospatiale Caravelle

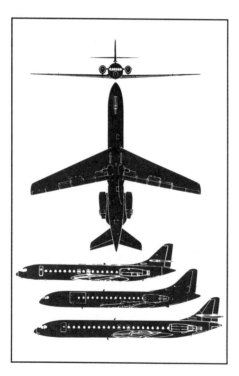

Nation: France

Versions: Series I, IA, III, VI-N, VI-R; Series 10R, 11R, 12, Super B (increasing size, capacity and range)

First flown: 1955

Length: 118.7ft (36.2m)   **Wingspan:** 112.5ft (34.3m)

Passenger capacity: 64-139

Cruising speed: 516mi (826km)/hr

Range: 1088-2165mi (1741-3464km)

Look-alikes: Caravelle has tailplanes which extend from much lower on the tailfin than *British Aerospace One-Eleven, Canadair Challenger/Regional Jet, Fokker F28/F100, Gulfstream Aerospace Gulfstream II/III/IV, McDonnell Douglas DC-9/MD-80,* and *Tupolev Tu-134.*

The first short-haul jet, and first jet designed with rear-mounted engines, the Caravelle was intended for travel between France and North Africa. In all, 279 were built. *Specs:* Caravelle 12; *Main silhouette:* Caravelle 11R; *Top/bottom side view silhouettes:* Caravelle 6R and 12; *Photo:* Caravelle 12.

Photo courtesy Aérospatiale

British Aerospace One-Eleven

Nation: United Kingdom

Versions: Series 200, 300, 475, 500 (increasingly stretched fuselages)

First flown: 1963

Length: 106.9ft (32.6m)   **Wingspan:** 93.5ft (28.5m)

Passenger capacity: 89-119

Cruising speed: 541mi (866km)/hr

Range: 2165mi (3464km)

Look-alikes: *Aérospatiale Caravelle* has tailplanes extending from much lower on the tailfin than One-Eleven. *Tupolev Tu-134* is flown only by airlines of former Eastern bloc countries. *McDonnell Douglas DC-9/MD-80* have a rear fuselage which tapers to a much sharper point than One-Eleven. *Gulfstream II/III/IV* and *Canadair Challenger/Regional Jet* are much smaller than One-Eleven. One-Eleven has a nose which tapers to a slimmer point and tailplanes which extend from slightly higher on the tailfin than on *Fokker F28/F100*.

A total of 252 One-Elevens have been built. U.K. production has ceased but, supplied by British Aerospace in kits, the One-Eleven is still assembled in Romania. *Specs:* Series 500; *Main silhouette:* Series 500; *Upper side view silhouette:* Series 400; *Photo:* Series 200.

Photo courtesy British Aerospace

Canadair Challenger/Regional Jet

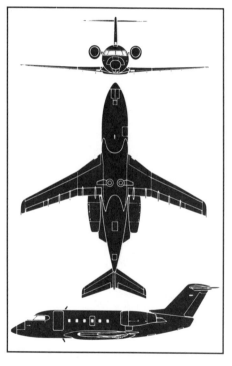

Nation: Canada

Versions: Challenger 600, 601 (new engines, winglets), Regional Jet (stretched fuselage)

First flown: 1978

Length: 88.6ft (27.0m)   **Wingspan:** 70.2ft (21.4m)

Passenger capacity: 19-50

Cruising speed: 539mi (862km)/hr

Range: 1633mi (2613km)

Look-alikes: Challenger/Regional Jet and *Gulfstream II/III/IV* are much smaller than other similar appearing planes. Challenger/Regional Jet have engines which are shorter in relation to the fuselage than those on *Gulfstream II/III/IV*.

The original Challenger was designed as an executive jet or commuter airliner. It was the first commercial jetliner built in Canada. The updated Regional Jet has a larger passenger capacity and longer range. *Specs:* Regional Jet; *Silhouette:* Challenger 600; *Photo:* Regional Jet.

Photo courtesy Canadair

Fokker F28/F100

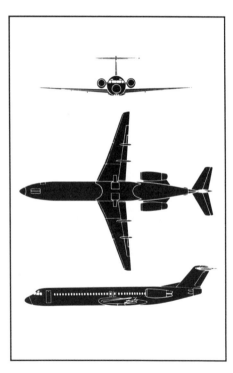

Nation: Netherlands

Versions: F28-1000 through -6000 (stretched fuselages and/or improved wings); F100 (19ft longer than longest F28 version with updated technology)

First flown: (F28) 1967; (F100) 1986

Length: (F100) 116.8ft (35.6m)   **Wingspan:** 92.2ft (28.1m)

Passenger capacity: (F28) 55-85; (F100) 110

Cruising speed: (F28) 419mi (670km)/hr; (F100) 468mi (748km)/hr

Range: (F28) 1151mi (1841km); (F100) 1767mi (2827km)

Look-alikes: *Aérospatiale Caravelle* has tailplanes which extend from much lower on the tailfin than F28/F100. *Tupolev Tu-134* is flown only by airlines of former Eastern bloc countries. *Gulfstream II/III/IV* and *Canadair Challenger/Regional Jet* are much smaller than F28/F100. *McDonnell Douglas DC-9/MD-80* have a tail which tapers to a much sharper point and tailfins with a different shape than F28/F100. *British Aerospace One-Eleven's* tailfins are a different shape and tailplanes attach slightly lower on tailfin compared to F28/F100.

This short to medium range airliner is in extensive use worldwide. A total of 241 F28's had been produced by 1986, when the model was replaced by the F100. *Silhouette:* F100; *Photo:* F28.

Photo courtesy Fokker Aircraft U.S.A.

Gulfstream Aerospace Gulfstream II/III/IV

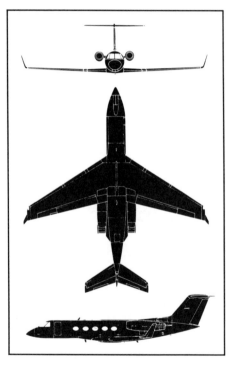

Nation: United States

Versions: Gulfstream II, III (stretched fuselage, winglets), IV (technologically advanced)

First flown: 1966

Length: 80.0ft (24.4m)   **Wingspan:** 68.9ft (21.0m)

Passenger capacity: 14-19

Cruising speed: 581mi (930km)/hr

Range: 3744mi (5990km)

Look-alikes: *Gulfstream II/III/IV* and *Canadair Challenger/ Regional Jet* are much smaller than other planes in this group. *Challenger/Regional Jet* have engines which are shorter in relation to the fuselage than those on Gulfstream II/III/IV.

T he Gulfstream is a large executive transport, designed for luxury travel. Gulfstream II's have been adapted as flying simulators for the American space shuttle astronauts. *Specs:* Gulfstream II; *Silhouette:* Gulfstream III; *Photo:* Gulfstream II.

Photo courtesy Gulfstream

McDonnell Douglas DC-9/MD-80

Nation: United States

Versions: DC-9 Series 10, 20, 30, 40, 50 (increasing size); MD-80, -81, -82, -83, -87, -88 (stretched fuselage, advanced engines and technology)

First flown: (DC-9) 1965; (MD-80) 1979

Length: (MD-80) 135.5ft (41.3m)   **Wingspan:** 107.9ft (32.9m)

Passenger capacity: (DC-9) 90-139; (MD-80) 172

Cruising speed: (DC-9) 564mi (902km)/hr; (MD-80) 589mi (942km)/hr

Range: (DC-9) 1335mi (2136km); (MD-80) 1810mi (2896km)

Look-alikes: DC-9/MD-80 have a tail which tapers to a much sharper point than *Fokker F28/F100* or *British Aerospace One-Eleven*. *Aérospatiale Caravelle* has tailplanes which extend from much lower on the tailfin than DC-9/MD-80. *Tupolev Tu-134* is flown only by airlines of former Eastern bloc countries. *Gulfstream II/III/IV* and *Canadair Challenger/Regional Jet* are much smaller than DC-9/MD-80.

The original DC-9 was designed to accommodate 75 passengers, while the current production versions, designated MD-80 and onwards, can carry up to 172 passengers. A total of 976 DC-9's were built, making it the most successful of twin jet, rear-engine commercial transports. *Silhouette: MD-80; Photo: DC-9-20.*

Photo courtesy Continental Airlines

Tupolev Tu-134

Nation: Russia

Versions: Tu-134; Tu-134A (stretched fuselage); Tu-134B, B-1, B-3 (internal modifications)

First flown: 1962

Length: 121.7ft (37.1m)   **Wingspan:** 95.1ft (29.0m)

Passenger capacity: 64-80

Cruising speed: 550mi (880km)/hr

Range: 1876mi (3002km)

Look-alikes: Tu-134 can be distinguished from planes similar in appearance by the fact that it is flown only by airlines of former Eastern bloc countries.

A short to medium range jetliner, the Tu-134 is a scaled down version of a Soviet bomber, the Tu-16. *Specs:* Tu-134A; *Silhouette:* Tu-134A; *Photo:* Tu-134A.

Photo courtesy Lot Polish Airlines

Boeing 727

Nation: United States

Versions: 727-100, 727-200 (stretched fuselage), 727-100C (passenger/cargo with side loading freight door), 727F (freighter)

First flown: 1963

Length: 153.2ft (46.7m)   **Wingspan:** 107.9ft (32.9m)

Passenger capacity: 145-189

Cruising speed: 573mi (917km)/hr

Range: 1670-2663mi (2672-4260km)

Look-alikes: Boeing 727 is flown throughout the world except by airlines of former Eastern bloc nations, while *Tupolev Tu-154* and *Yakovlev Yak-42* are flown only by airlines of former Eastern bloc countries.

With 1,832 built and production ending in 1984, the Boeing 727 is one of the most successful commercial jet transports. It is the only rear engine jetliner built by Boeing Aircraft. *Specs: 727-200; Main silhouette: 727-200; Upper side view silhouette: 727-100; Photo: 727-100.*

Photo courtesy Boeing

Tupolev Tu-154

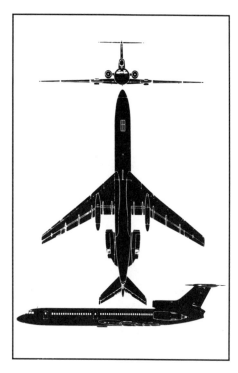

Nation: Russia

Versions: Tu-154A to M (improved avionics and engines, higher seating capacity), Tu-154C (freighter)

First flown: 1968

Length: 157.1ft (47.9m)   **Wingspan:** 123.3ft (37.6m)

Passenger capacity: 168-180

Cruising speed: 590mi (944km)/hr

Range: 2423-4100mi (3877-6560km)

Look-alikes: Tu-154 and *Yakovlev Yak-42* are flown only by airlines of former Eastern bloc countries or Egypt, while *Boeing* 727 is flown throughout the world except by airlines of former Eastern bloc nations. Tu-154 is much longer than *Yak-42*.

The Soviet equivalent of the Boeing 727, this plane entered service approximately five years after the 727. Operated by airlines of former Eastern bloc countries and Egypt, it can take off from and land on rough airfields with short runways. *Specs:* Tu-154B; *Silhouette:* Tu-154M; *Photo:* Tu-154M.

Photo courtesy Lot Polish Airlines

All jets on tail

Yakovlev Yak-42

Nation: Russia

Versions: Yak-42, Yak-42M (higher capacity, stretched fuselage)

First flown: 1975

Length: 119.4ft (36.4m)   **Wingspan:** 114.5ft (34.9m)

Passenger capacity: 104-168

Cruising speed: 503mi (805km)/hr

Range: 1250mi (2000km)

Look-alikes: *Boeing 727* is flown throughout the world except by airlines of former Eastern bloc nations, while *Tupolev Tu-154* and Yak-42 are flown only by airlines of former Eastern bloc countries. *Tu-154* is much longer than Yak-42.

The Yak-42 was developed as a short-haul, medium capacity transport with the ability to operate in remote areas of the former Soviet Union with a minimum of maintenance.

Photo courtesy Smithsonian Institution

All jets on tail

British Aerospace VC10

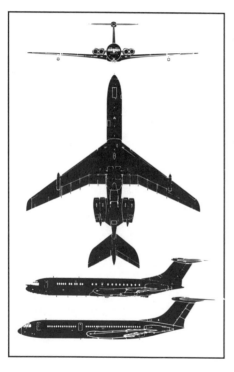

Nation: United Kingdom

Versions: VC10, Super VC10 (stretched fuselage and greater range)

First flown: 1962

Length: 171.5ft (52.3m)   **Wingspan:** 146.3ft (44.6m)

Passenger capacity: 150-174

Cruising speed: 581mi (930km)/hr

Range: 3922mi (6275km)

Look-alikes: VC10 and *Ilyushin IL-62* are unique in having paired jet engines on either side of the rear fuselage. VC10 is currently in service only with the Royal Air Force (U.K.), while *IL-62* is flown only by airlines of former Eastern bloc countries.

The VC10 is in service with the Royal Air Force in the capacity of a passenger, cargo, and fuel transport. As a tanker, it is capable of in-flight refuelling of other planes. *Specs:* Super VC10; *Main silhouette:* VC10; *Lower side view silhouette:* Super VC10; *Photo:* Super VC10.

Ilyushin IL-62

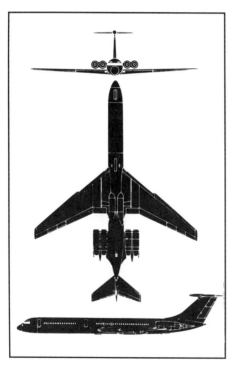

Nation: Russia

Versions: IL-62M (new engines, improved equipment, larger fuel capacity), IL-62MK (increased capacity)

First flown: 1963

Length: 174.2ft (53.1m)   **Wingspan:** 141.7ft (43.2m)

Passenger capacity: 186

Cruising speed: 575mi (920km)/hr

Range: 4857mi (7771km)

Look-alikes: IL-62 and *British Aerospace VC10* are unique in having paired jet engines on either side of the rear fuselage. *VC10* is currently in service only with the Royal Air Force (U.K.), while IL-62 is flown only by airlines of former Eastern bloc countries.

The IL-62 and BAe VC10 are the world's only rear engine four jet airliners. Aeroflot flies most of the 230 IL-62's currently in service. *Specs:* IL-62M; *Silhouette:* IL-62M; *Photo:* IL-62M.

Photo courtesy Lot Polish Airlines

Propeller airplanes with 4 propeller engines on wings

If the plane looks generally like this, with 2 engines on each wing, and the wings extending from low on the fuselage, go to pages 68 to 77.

If the plane looks generally like this, with 2 engines on each wing, and the wings extending from high on the fuselage, go to pages 78 to 83.

Aero/Boeing Spacelines Guppy

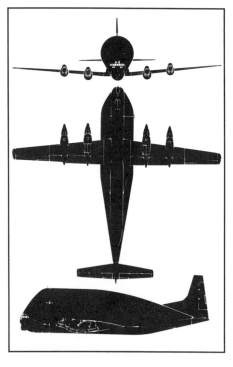

Nations: United States, France

Versions: Guppy; Pregnant, Super, and Mini-Guppy (varying sizes)

First flown: 1962

Length: 144.7ft (43.8m)   **Wingspan:** 156.1ft (47.6m)

Freight capacity: 54,000lb (24,545kg)

Cruising speed: 288mi (461km)/hr

Range: 508-2938mi (813-4700km)

Look-alikes: The unique shape of its very large fuselage distinguishes Guppy from all other airplanes.

The unique and unmistakable design of the Guppy was derived from the Boeing 377 Stratocruiser airliner. Retaining the 377's wings and engines, the fuselage was modified and greatly enlarged. Designed to accommodate outsize loads of cargo, it was used by NASA to transport large sections of rockets for the U.S. space program and is currently employed by Airbus to move sections of airliner fuselage between manufacturing centers in Europe. *Specs:* Guppy; *Silhouette:* Guppy; *Photo:* Super Guppy.

Photo courtesy Airbus Industrie

Douglas DC-4/C-54 Skymaster

Nation: United States

Versions: DC-4, C-54 (military version)

First flown: 1938

Length: 93.8ft (28.6m)   **Wingspan:** 117.4ft (35.8m)

Passenger capacity: 44-86

Cruising speed: 207mi (331km)/hr

Range: 2500mi (4000km)

Look-alikes: *Lockheed Electra* has tailfins with a shape different from that on DC-4. *Douglas DC-6/DC-7* have a nose which tapers to a sharper point than DC-4. *Vickers Viscount* has tailplanes which are more steeply upwardly pitched than on DC-4. *Aero Spacelines Guppy* has a very large and uniquely shaped fuselage.

M ore than 200 DC-4's originated as C-54's for military use in World War II. The U.S. Air Force initiated the first regular freight service across the North Atlantic using C-54's, and one served as President Roosevelt's personal aircraft. After the war many were released to civilian service, and Douglas produced another 79 intended specifically for commercial use.

Photo courtesy Harry Gann/McDonnell Douglas

Douglas DC-6/DC-7

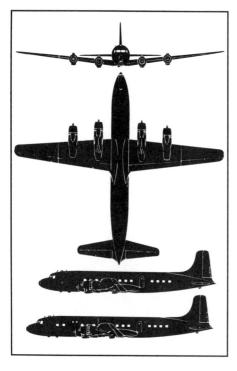

Nation: United States

Versions: DC-6, DC-6A and B (stretched fuselage), DC-7 (further stretched fuselage), DC-7B (longer range), DC-7C (maximally stretched fuselage and extended wing), DC-7F (freighter)

First flown: (DC-6) 1946; (DC-7) 1953

Length: (DC-6B) 105.6ft (32.2m)   **Wingspan:** 117.4ft (35.8m)

Passenger capacity: (DC-6) 48-102; (DC-7) 60-95

Cruising speed: (DC-6B) 315mi (504km)/hr; (DC-7C) 355mi (568km)/hr

Range: (DC-6B) 3005mi (4808km); (DC-7C) 4705mi (7528km)

Look-alikes: DC-6/DC-7 are larger than and have a nose which tapers to a sharper point than *Lockheed L-188 Electra, Douglas DC-4/C-54*, and *Vickers Viscount. Aero Spacelines Guppy* has a very large and uniquely shaped fuselage.

Derived from the DC-4, the DC-6 has a pressurized cabin, longer fuselage, and increased range. A stretch version of the DC-6, the DC-7B achieved intercontinental range and was designed for non-stop North Atlantic operations. The DC-7C inaugerated transpolar passenger flights, first flying between Tokyo and Copenhagen in 1957. The C-118 military version is still used by armed forces around the globe. *Main silhouette:* DC-6B; *Upper side view silhouette:* DC-6; *Photo:* DC-7C.

Photo courtesy Harry Gann/McDonnell Douglas

Four prop engines on wings

Lockheed L-188 Electra

Nation: United States

Versions: L-188A, L-188C (longer range), P-3 Orion (anti-submarine military version)

First flown: 1957

Length: 104.3ft (31.8m)   **Wingspan:** 99.1ft (30.2m)

Passenger capacity: 66-99

Cruising speed: 405mi (648km)/hr

Range: 2770mi (4432km)

Look-alikes: Electra has tailfins which extend from higher on the fuselage than *McDonnell Douglas DC-4, DC-6* and *DC-7*. *Vickers Viscount* is smaller than Electra, and has steeply upwardly pitched tailplanes. *Aero Spacelines Guppy* has a very large and uniquely shaped fuselage.

In the first years of its operation the Electra suffered two disastrous crashes, eventually found to have resulted from metal fatigue. As a result, structural modifications were made to the wings. The Electra is mainly in use today as a commercial freighter. A military derivative is the P-3 Orion anti-submarine aircraft, distinguishable by the absence of cabin windows and a boom extending from the rear of the fuselage.

Photo courtesy Lockheed Aircraft

Vickers Viscount

Nation: United Kingdom

Versions: Series 700, 700D, 770D, 800, 810 (increasing payload, stretched fuselage, cabin improvements)

First flown: 1948

Length: 85.6ft (26.1m)   **Wingspan:** 93.8ft (28.6m)

Passenger capacity: 47-71

Cruising speed: 357mi (571km)/hr

Range: 1725mi (2760km)

Look-alikes: Viscount is smaller than *Lockheed Electra* and has steeply upwardly pitched tailplanes. *McDonnell Douglas DC-6/DC-7* are larger than and have a tailfin shaped differently from Viscount's. Viscount's tailplanes are more steeply upwardly pitched than those on *Douglas DC-4/C-54*. *Aero Spacelines Guppy* has a very large and uniquely shaped fuselage.

The he world's first commercial turboprop, the Viscount is still in service in many countries both as a passenger plane and freighter. A total of 440 were built through 1964. *Specs:* 810; *Main silhouette:* 800; *Upper side view silhouette:* 700; *Photo:* 700.

Photo courtesy Vickers Aircraft

Four prop engines on wings

Antonov An-12

Nation: Ukraine

First flown: 1957

Length: 108.6ft (33.1m)   **Wingspan:** 124.6ft (38.0m)

Passenger capacity: 84-100

Cruising speed: 419mi (670km)/hr

Range: 3563mi (5700km)

Look-alikes: *Lockheed C-130/L-100* has a nose which tapers to a slimmer point than that of An-12, which is seen only in the markings of airlines of the republics of the former Soviet Union or its client states. *de Havilland DHC Dash-7* is a much smaller plane than An-12.

A very numerous Soviet transport, the An-12 is used extensively both in military and civilian roles. Similar in appearance to the American C-130, it has been exported to many countries including the People's Republic of China, Bulgaria, Cuba, Iraq, Poland, and Guinea.

Photo courtesy Smithsonian Institution

de Havilland DHC Dash-7

Nation: Canada

Versions: Series 100, Series 101 (freighter), Series 150 (increased payload), Series 151 (freighter version of Series 150)

First flown: 1975

Length: 80.4ft (24.5m)   **Wingspan:** 93.2ft (28.4m)

Passenger capacity: 50-54

Cruising speed: 266mi (426km)/hr

Range: 846mi (1354km)

Look-alikes: Dash-7 has tailplanes extending from high on the tailfin, compared to much lower on *Antonov An-12* and *Lockheed C-130/L-100*.

D esigned for use at close-in downtown city airports, the Dash-7 is exceptionally quiet and capable of take-off and landing from runways as short as 2000 feet. Well over 100 have been ordered. *Specs:* Series 100; *Silhouette:* Series 100; *Photo:* Series 100.

Photo courtesy Tony Honeywood/de Havilland Inc. Boeing Canada

Lockheed C-130 Hercules/L-100

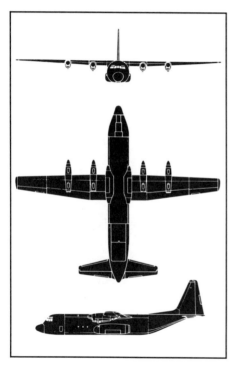

Nation: United States

Versions: Many tailored to specific tasks

First flown: 1954

Length: 112.8ft (34.4m)   **Wingspan:** 132.5ft (40.4m)

Passenger capacity: 79-100

Cruising speed: 355mi (568km)/hr

Range: 1841-5562mi (2945-8899km)

Look-alikes: C-130/L-100 have a nose which tapers to a slimmer point than that of *Antonov An-12*, which is seen only in the markings of airlines of the republics of the former Soviet Union or its client states. *de Havilland DHC Dash-7* is a much smaller plane than C-130/L-100.

One of the most numerous military transports built in the West, the many variants of the C-130 have been adapted to such uses as troop transport (C-130H), tanker (C130F), gunship (AC-130E), and communications (EC-130). The L-100 is the civilian variant. *Specs:* L-100; *Silhouette:* L-100; *Photo:* C-130.

Photo courtesy U.S. Air Force

Propeller airplanes with 2 engines on wings; Wings extend from low on the fuselage

If the plane looks generally like this, with tailplanes extending from the fuselage, go to pages 86 to 103.

British Aerospace 748/ATP.....p. 86
Convair 240-640.....p. 88
Curtiss C-46 Commando.....p. 90
Douglas DC-3.....p. 92
Embraer EMB-110.....p. 94
Gulfstream Aerospace Gulfstream I/I-C.....p. 96
Ilyushin IL-14.....p. 98
Martin 4-0-4.....p. 100
Saab 340.....p. 102

If the plane looks generally like this, with tailplanes extending from the tailfin below its top, go to pages 104 to 107.

British Aerospace Jetstream 31.....p. 104
Fairchild Metro.....p. 106

If the plane looks generally like this, with tailplanes extending from the top of tailfin, go to pages 108 to 111.

Beechcraft 1900C.....p. 108
Embraer EMB-120 Brasilia.....p. 110

British Aerospace 748/ATP

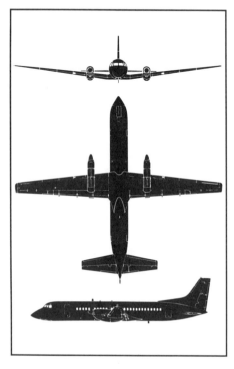

Nation: United Kingdom

Versions: 748, Super 748 (improved engines), ATP (advanced technology with stretched fuselage)

First flown: (748) 1960; (ATP) 1986

Length: (ATP) 85.3ft (26.0m)   **Wingspan:** 100.4ft (30.6m)

Passenger capacity: (748) 40-58; (ATP) 60-72

Cruising speed: (748) 282mi (451km)/hr; (ATP) 306mi (489km)/hr

Range: (748) 1159mi (1854km); (ATP) 2153mi (3444km)

Look-alikes: *Convair 240-640, Curtiss Commando,* and *Douglas DC-3* have differently shaped tailfins from 748/ATP. *Martin 4-0-4* has a tailfin which extends much further forward on the fuselage than 748/ATP. *Gulfstream Aerospace Gulfstream I/I-C* and *Saab 340* have tailplanes which pitch upward from the fuselage compared to 748/ATP. *Embraer EMB-110* is much smaller with a very differently shaped fuselage. *Ilyushin IL-14* is flown only by airlines of former Eastern bloc countries.

The 748 was designed in the 1950's as a replacement for the DC-3 and its contemporaries. Almost 400 748's were sold between 1961 and 1986 before the model was replaced by the ATP, a stretched derivative with updated engines. *Silhouette:* ATP; *Photo:* 748.

Photo courtesy British Aerospace

Convair 240, 340, 440, 540, 580, 600, 640

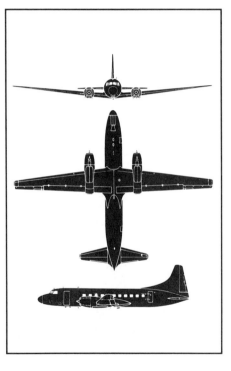

Nation: United States

Versions: Increased length of fuselage and replacement of piston engines with turboprops in versions 540 onwards

First flown: 1947

Length: 79.0ft (24.1m)   **Wingspan:** 105.3ft (32.1m)

Passenger capacity: 44-56

Cruising speed: 301mi (482km)/hr

Range: 1234mi (1974km)

Look-alikes: *British Aerospace 748/ATP, Douglas DC-3,* and *Gulfstream Aerospace Gulfstream I/I-C* have differently shaped tailfins from Convair. *Martin 4-0-4* has a tailfin which extends much further forward on the fuselage than Convair. *Curtiss Commando* has a much less prominent nose and tailplanes which extend from higher on the fuselage than Convair. *Saab 340* has tailplanes which pitch upwards from the fuselage compared to Convair. *Embraer EMB-110* is much smaller with a very differently shaped fuselage. *Ilyushin IL-14* is flown only by airlines of former Eastern bloc countries.

Evolving over 21 years of production, early improvements included lengthening the fuselage, while versions from the 540 onwards incorporated turboprop engine technology. Variants were produced for the U.S. military to serve as air ambulances, freighters, and for training purposes. *Specs:* 640; *Silhouette:* 340; *Photo:* 340.

Photo courtesy General Dynamics

Two props with wings low on fuselage

Curtiss C-46 Commando

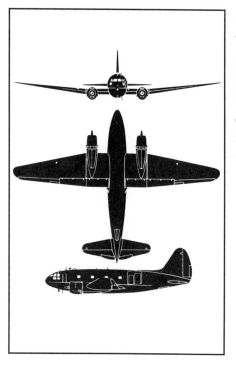

Nation: United States

Versions: C-46 and C-55 (military), CW-20 (commercial)

First flown: 1940

Length: 76.4ft (23.3m)   **Wingspan:** 107.9ft (32.9m)

Passenger capacity: 36-62

Cruising speed: 187mi (299km)/hr

Range: 1170mi (1872km)

Look-alikes: Commando has the least prominent nose of all otherwise similar planes—note that its nose does not taper from the line of the fuselage when viewed in profile.

O riginally designed as a pressurized 36 passenger aircraft in 1937, the C-46 served extensively as a World War II military transport and could accommodate 40 fully equipped troops. A total of 3,180 were built. Adapted to civilian use after the end of the war, the C-46, like its look-alike, the DC-3, has remained in continuous use to the present day.

Photo courtesy Air Manitoba

Douglas DC-3

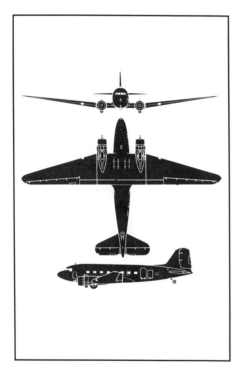

Nation: United States

Versions: DC-3 A and B (improved engines); many military versions including C-47; Lisunov Li-2 (produced under license in Soviet Union); L2D (under license in Japan)

First flown: 1935

Length: 64.6ft (19.7m)   **Wingspan:** 95.1ft (29.0m)

Passenger capacity: 21-36

Cruising speed: 226mi (362km)/hr

Range: 1519mi (2430km)

Look-alikes: *British Aerospace 748/ATP* and *Convair 240-640* have differently shaped tailfins from DC-3. *Convair 240-640* also have a more prominent nose than DC-3. *Martin 4-0-4* has a tailfin which extends further forward on the fuselage than DC-3. *Curtiss C-46 Commando* has a much less prominent nose than DC-3. *Gulfstream I/I-C* and *Saab 340* have tailplanes which pitch steeply upwards from the fuselage. *Embraer EMB-110* is much smaller with a very differently shaped fuselage. *Ilyushin IL-14* is flown only by airlines of former Eastern bloc countries.

Perhaps the most celebrated of all transports, the DC-3 is also the most prolificly produced airplane of all time. More than 12,000 were produced, many for service in World War II. Eisenhower considered the DC-3 one of the four most significant weapons in the war. Conversion of military models provided the backbone of most airline fleets in the immediate post-war period. Several hundred are still in use.

Photo courtesy Harry Gann/McDonnell Douglas

Embraer EMB-110 Bandeirante

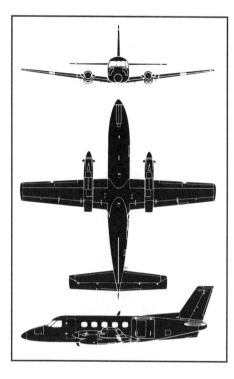

Nation: Brazil

Versions: 12 versions adapted for specific military/civilian uses

First flown: 1968

Length: 50.2ft (15.3m)   **Wingspan:** 49.5ft (15.1m)

Passenger capacity: 21

Cruising speed: 259mi (414km)/hr

Range: 1180mi (1888km)

Look-alikes: All similar looking planes except *Saab 340* are much larger than EMB-110. In contrast to the EMB-110, the *Saab 340* has steeply upwardly pitched tailplanes.

The successful first product of Embraer (Empresa Brasileira de Aeronautica), the EMB-110 was designed in many versions for the Brazilian military. Hundreds have been sold to airlines around the world as a commuter transport.

Photo courtesy Embraer

Grumman Gulfstream I/I-C

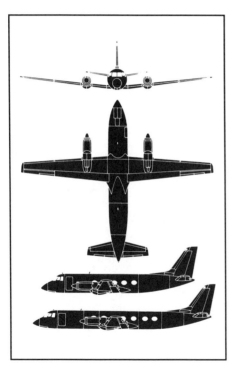

Nation: United States

Versions: I, I-C (stretched fuselage)

First flown: 1958

Length: 63.6ft (19.4m)   **Wingspan:** 78.4ft (23.9m)

Passenger capacity: 24-37

Cruising speed: 350mi (560km)/hr

Range: 2555mi (4088km)

Look-alikes: Gulfstream I/I-C and *Saab 340* have tailplanes which pitch upward from the fuselage, distinguishing them from airplanes otherwise similar in appearance. In addition to having tailplanes which are less steeply upwardly pitched than on Saab 340, Gulfstream I/I-C have a tailfin which is different in shape.

The Gulfstream I was designed as a business plane, while the I-C, with extended fuselage and increased capacity, is intended as a commuter aircraft. Originating with the Grumman American Aviation Corporation, rights for the Gulfstream were obtained by American Jet Industries in 1978, when Grumman American was purchased from its parent Grumman Corporation. *Specs:* Gulfstream I; *Main silhouette:* Gulfstream I; *Lower side view silhouette:* Gulfstream I-C; *Photo:* Gulfstream I.

Photo courtesy Grumman Aircraft

Ilyushin IL-14

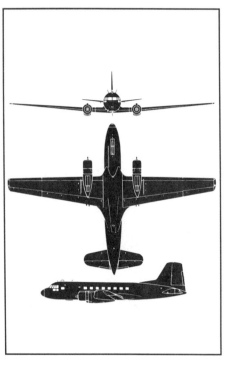

Nation: Russia

First flown: 1952

Length: 73.1ft (22.3m) **Wingspan:** 104.0ft (31.7m)

Passenger capacity: 18-42

Cruising speed: 198mi (317km)/hr

Range: 2000mi (3202km)

Look-alikes: IL-14 wears the markings of airlines of the Eastern European and former Soviet republics, distinguishing it from all other planes of similar appearance.

Most of the remaining IL-14's are operated in the People's Republic of China, with some in North Korea and Eastern Europe. Versions of this DC-3 look-alike were built in East Germany and Czechoslovakia.

Photo courtesy Smithsonian Institution

Martin 4-0-4

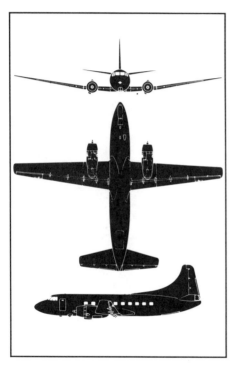

Nation: United States

Versions: 2-0-2, 3-0-3, 4-0-4 (progressive technical improvements including pressurized cabin)

First flown: (202) 1946; (404) 1950

Length: 74.8ft (22.8m)   **Wingspan:** 93.2ft (28.4m)

Passenger capacity: 44-56

Cruising speed: 280mi (448km)/hr

Range: 1080mi (1728km)

Look-alikes: 4-0-4 has a tailfin which extends much further forward on its fuselage than other planes of similar appearance.

Developed by the Martin company after World War II, the Martin 2-0-2 was intended to surpass the pre-war Douglas DC-3 and Curtiss Commando in performance. In comparison to the 2-0-2, the 4-0-4 has a longer fuselage and a pressurized cabin. Production problems and a wing failure which led to a crash limited its success, but a few of the 4-0-4's are still in service.

Two props with wings low on fuselage

Saab 340

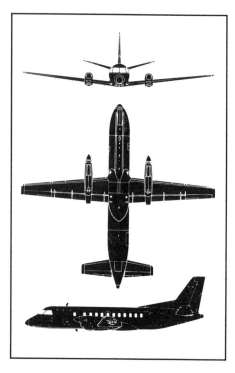

Nation: Sweden

Versions: 340A, 340B (more powerful engines, larger tailplanes, extended range)

First flown: 1983

Length: 64.6ft (19.7m)   **Wingspan** 70.2ft (21.4m)

Passenger capacity: 35

Cruising speed: 313mi (501km)/hr

Range: 1082mi (1731km)

Look-alikes: Saab 340 and *Gulfstream I/I-C* have tailplanes which pitch upward from the fuselage, distinguishing them from other planes of similar appearance. In addition to having tailplanes which are more steeply upwardly pitched than *Gulfstream I/I-C,* Saab 340 has a tailfin which is different in shape.

Originally a joint project with the U.S. firm Fairchild, the 340 is now made only by Saab. A larger version, the 2000, is planned for delivery in 1993. *Specs:* 340A; *Silhouette:* 340A; *Photo:* 340A.

Photo courtesy Saab

British Aerospace Jetstream 31

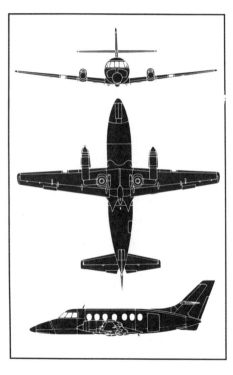

Nation: United Kingdom

First flown: 1967

Length: 47.2ft (14.4m)   **Wingspan:** 52.2ft (15.9m)

Passenger capacity: 19

Cruising speed: 266mi (426km)/hr

Range: 1234mi (1975km)

Look-alikes: Jetstream 31 can be distinguished from *Fairchild Metro* by tailplanes which extend from higher on the tailfin and which are not swept back. It also has a less prominent nose than *Metro*.

The Jetstream was originally manufactured by Handley Page and then by Scottish Aviation, which was in turn absorbed by British Aerospace. It serves the executive, commuter, and military markets.

Photo courtesy British Aerospace

Fairchild Metro

Nation: United States

Versions: Metro, Metro III (longer wing), Metro IVA (business), Expediter (cargo)

First flown: 1969

Length: 59.4ft (18.1m)   **Wingspan:** 57.1ft (17.4m)

Passenger capacity: 19

Cruising speed: 288mi (460km)/hr

Range: 1006mi (1610km)

Look-alikes: Metro is different from *British Aerospace Jetstream 31* in having tailplanes which extend from lower on the tailfin and which are swept back. It also has a more prominent nose than *Jetstream 31.*

With more than 350 built, the Metro was one of the most successful of a class of regional airliners designed to carry up to 19 passengers. This is the largest capacity plane allowed by FAA regulations to be operated without a cabin attendant. *Specs:* Metro III; *Silhouette:* Metro III; *Photo:* Metro III.

Beechcraft 1900C

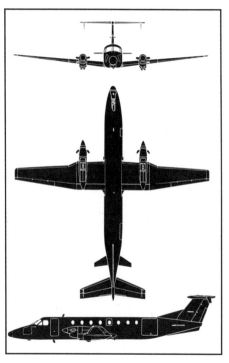

Nation: United States

Versions: 1900C (passenger/cargo), 1900C Exec-liner (business), C-12J (military)

First flown: 1982

Length: 57.7ft (17.6m)   **Wingspan:** 54.4ft (16.6m)

Passenger capacity: 19

Cruising speed: 310mi (496km)/hr

Range: 1490mi (2384km)

Look-alikes: The tail-lets which extend down from the tailplanes and the small horizontal tail surfaces extending from the rear of the fuselage distinguish the Beechcraft 1900C from the *Embraer EMB-120.*

n competition with the more successful Fairchild Metro, this regional airliner was designed with a capacity of 19 passengers, the maximum allowed by FAA regulations without a cabin attendant.

Photo courtesy Continental Airlines

Two props with wings low on fuselage

Embraer EMB-120

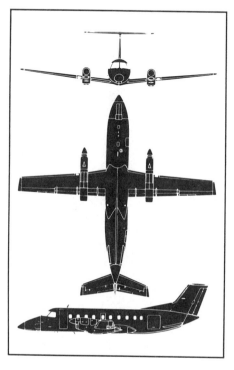

Nation: Brazil

Versions: cargo and military versions for Brazilian armed forces

First flown: 1983

Length: 65.6ft (20.0m)   **Wingspan:** 64.9ft (19.8m)

Passenger capacity: 18-30

Cruising speed: 343mi (549km)/hr

Range: 1864mi (2982km)

Look-alikes: In contrast to the *Beechcraft 1900C,* the EMB-120 lacks the distinctive tail-lets which extend down from the tailplane and the small horizontal tail surfaces extending from the rear of the fuselage.

A fter the success of the EMB-110, Embraer embarked on development of the larger and more ambitious EMB-120. An unusual example of a commercially successful transport built by a developing country, the EMB-120 is in use with airlines in both North America and Europe.

Photo courtesy Embraer

Propeller airplanes with 2 engines on wings;
Wings extend from high on the fuselage

If the plane looks like this, with tailplanes extending from the lower part of the tailfin or from the fuselage, go to pages 114 to 127.

If the plane looks like this, with tailplanes attached at or near the top of the tailfin, go to pages 128 to 131.

If the plane looks like this, with twin tailfins and a box-like fuselage, go to pages 132 to 135.

Two props with wings high on fuselage

Aérospatiale N 262

Nation: France

Versions: A, B, C, D (engine variations); Mohawk 298 (new engines and updated technology for use in the U.S.)

First flown: 1962

Length: 63.3ft (19.3m)   **Wingspan:** 74.1ft (22.6m)

Passenger capacity: 26-29

Cruising speed: 246mi (394km)/hr

Range: 593mi (949km)

Look-alikes: N 262, *Airtech CN-235, Dornier Do 228* and *Shorts 360* are identified by landing gear pods of various shapes and sizes protruding from the lower part of their fuselages under the wings. *CN-235* has a less prominent nose than N 262, while *Do 228* has a much more prominent nose. *Shorts 360* has a box shaped fuselage with a flat upper surface in contrast to N 262.

A short haul airliner. Of 110 built and sold throughout the world, approximately 20 remain in use by airlines. Some are also in service with the French Air Force. *Silhouette:* Series C; *Photo:* Mohawk 298.

Photo courtesy Aérospatiale

Airtech CN-235

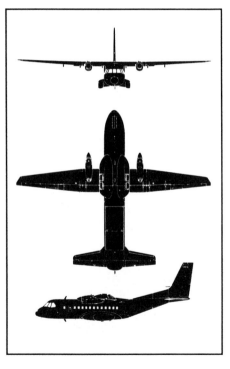

Nations: Spain, Indonesia

Versions: Series 10, Series 100 (upgraded engines)

First flown: 1983

Length: 70.2ft (21.4m)   **Wingspan:** 84.6ft (25.8m)

Passenger capacity: 45

Cruising speed: 281mi (450km)/hr

Range: 2445mi (3912km)

Look-alikes: CN-235, *Aérospatiale N 262, Dornier Do 228,* and *Shorts 360* are identified by landing gear pods of various shapes and sizes protruding from the lower part of their fuselages under the wings. *N 262* and *Do 228* have more prominent noses than the CN-235. *Shorts 360* has a box shaped fuselage with a flat upper surface in contrast to N 262.

A joint effort of aircraft companies in Spain (Construcciones Aeronauticas SA) and Indonesia (I.P.T.N.), the CN-235 was designed for both military and civilian use. Sales of the plane have been evenly split between these two applications.

Photo courtesy CASA

Antonov An-24/An-26

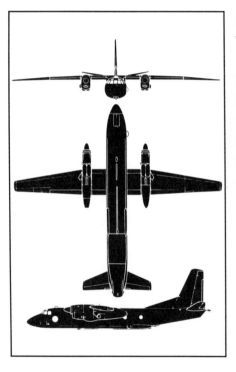

Nation: Ukraine

Versions: An-24, An-24V (50 passengers), An-24T and RT (freighters), An-26 (re-designed rear fuselage and new engines)

First flown: 1960

Length: 77.1ft (23.5m)   **Wingspan:** 95.8ft (29.2m)

Passenger capacity: 44-52

Cruising speed: 280mi (448km)/hr

Range: 1500mi (2400km)

Look-alikes: Antonov An-24/An-26 are usually seen in the markings of airlines of former Eastern bloc countries or client states of the former Soviet Union, distinguishing them from other planes of similar appearance.

Designed as short-haul feeder planes for Aeroflot, the Soviet airline, over 1000 of these types were built. Extensively exported to Soviet allies and client states in Europe, Africa, and Asia, the An-24 is still produced in the People's Republic of China as the Y7-100. *Specs:* An-24; *Silhouette:* An-26; *Photo:* An-24.

Photo courtesy Lot Polish Airlines

Two props with wings high on fuselage

de Havilland DHC-6 Twin Otter

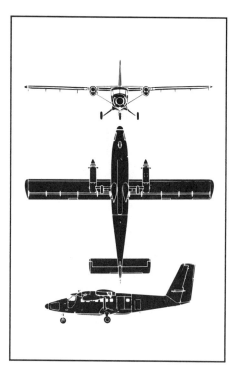

Nation: Canada

Versions: Series 100 (original), Series 200 (extended nose), Series 300 (externally identical to 200 with upgraded engines)

First flown: 1965

Length: 51.8ft (15.8m)   **Wingspan:** 64.9ft (19.8m)

Passenger capacity: 20

Cruising speed: 210mi (336km)/hr

Range: 1109mi (1775km)

Look-alikes: The tailplanes which extend from the lower portion of the tailfin distinguish Twin Otter from other planes of similar appearance, whose tailplanes extend either from close to the top of the tailfins or from close to the junction of the tailfin and fuselage. Non-retractable landing gear, a prominent nose, and small size are other identifying features.

A ble to operate from short, rough runways, the Twin Otter has been sold to airlines in more than 70 nations. It is also in use by the armed forces of Canada (CC-138) and the U.S. (UV-18). A floatplane variant differs in having a shortened nose and additional fins above and below the tailplanes. *Specs:* Series 300; *Silhouette:* Series 200; *Photo:* Series 300.

Photo courtesy Tony Honeywood/de Havilland Inc. Boeing Canada

Two props with wings high on fuselage

Dornier Do 228

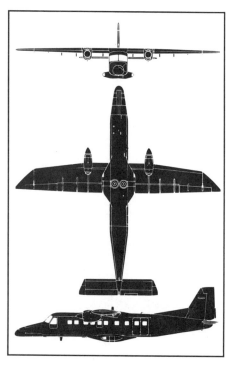

Nation: Germany

Versions: Do 228-100, Do 228-200 (stretched fuselage), Do 228-203F (freighter)

First flown: 1981

Length: 54.4ft (16.6m)   **Wingspan:** 55.8ft (17.0m)

Passenger capacity: 15-19

Cruising speed: 266mi (427km)/hr

Range: 1080mi (1728km)

Look-alikes: Do 228, *Aérospatiale N 262, Airtech CN-235,* and *Shorts 360* are identified by landing gear pods of various shapes and sizes protruding from the lower part of their fuselages under the wings. Do 228 has a more prominent nose than either the *N 262* or *CN-235.* In addition to a less prominent nose, *Shorts 360* has landing gear pods which are larger than those on Do 228.

The design of the Do 228 includes a uniquely shaped high technology wing. The model -200 is 11 feet longer than the -100, and in addition to increasing passenger capacity from 15 to 19, can fly more than twice as far. The Do 228 is produced in India under license by Hindustan Aeronautics. *Specs:* -200; *Silhouette:* -200; *Photo:* -200.

Photo courtesy Dornier Aviation

Fokker F27/F50

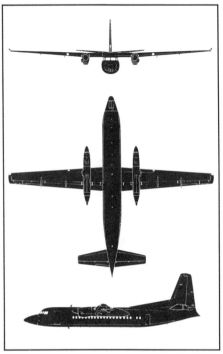

Nation: Netherlands

Versions: F27, F50 (virtually identical in external appearance to F27 with updated engines and technology)

First flown: (F27) 1955; (F50) 1985

Length: (F50) 82.7ft (25.2m)　　**Wingspan:** 95.1ft (29.0m)

Passenger capacity: (F27) 28-60; (F50) 50-58

Cruising speed: (F27) 298mi (477km)/hr; (F50) 324mi (518km)/hr

Range: (F27) 1382mi (2211km); (F50) 1864mi (2982km)

Look-alikes: *Airtech CN-235, Aérospatiale N 262, Dornier Do 228,* and *Shorts 360* all have landing gear pods of various shapes and sizes protruding from the lower part of their fuselages under the wings, absent from F27/F50. F27/F50 have a more prominent, tapered nose than *Antonov An-24/An-26,* usually seen in the markings of former Eastern bloc countries. *de Havilland Twin Otter* is a much smaller airplane than F27/F50 and has non-retractable landing gear and tailplanes extending from higher on the tailfin than F27/F50.

Almost 800 F27's were built before the design was supplanted by that of the F50 in 1985. Both F27 and F50 are in common use in Europe and North America as short-haul connectors for both passengers and freight. *Silhouette:* F50; *Photo:* F27.

Photo courtesy Fokker Aircraft U.S.A.

Shorts 360

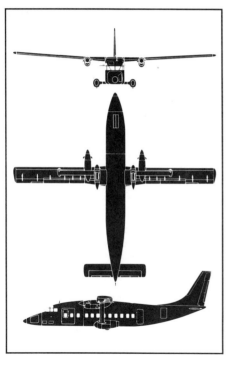

Nation: United Kingdom

Versions: 360, 360-300 (improved engines and cabin), 360-300F (freighter)

First flown: 1981

Length: 70.5ft (21.5m)   **Wingspan:** 74.8ft (22.8m)

Passenger capacity: 36

Cruising speed: 249mi (398km)/hr

Range: 997mi (1595km)

Look-alikes: Shorts 360, *Aérospatiale N 262*, *Airtech CN-235*, and *Dornier Do 228* all have landing gear pods of various shapes and sizes protruding from the lower part of their fuselages under the wings. The box-like fuselage and struts extending from the wings down to the landing gear pods distinguish Shorts 360 from these other planes.

The Shorts 360 is a re-design of the Shorts 330 with enlarged fuselage, a new tail, and improved engines. Changes made in U.S. airline regulations in 1978 allowed Shorts and other aircraft companies to design commuter planes larger than the previous 30 seat capacity. *Specs: 360-300; Silhouette: 360; Photo: 360-300.*

Photo courtesy Short Brothers

Avions de Transport Régional ATR 42/ATR 72

Nations: Italy, France

Versions: ATR 42-200 and -300 (passenger), ATR 42F (freighter), ATR 72 (stretched fuselage version of ATR 42)

First flown: (ATR42) 1984; (ATR72) 1985

Length: (ATR42) 74.5ft (22.7m)   **Wingspan:** 80.7ft (24.6m)

Passenger capacity: (ATR42) 42-50; (ATR72) 64-74

Cruising speed: (ATR42) 308mi (493km)/hr; (ATR72) 329mi (526km)/hr

Range: (ATR42) 1209mi (1934km); (ATR72) 1666mi (2666km)

Look-alikes: ATR 42/ATR 72 have landing gear pods protruding from the lower fuselage under the wings, absent on *de Havilland DHC-8 Dash-8*. In comparison to *Dash-8,* ATR 42/ATR 72 also have a differently shaped tailfin and a fuselage which extends further behind the tailfin.

Jointly developed by Aérospatiale of France and Aeritalia of Italy. Over 100 have been produced. *Main silhouette:* ATR 42; *Lower side view silhouette:* ATR 72; *Photo:* ATR 42.

Photo courtesy Continental Airlines

de Havilland DHC-8 Dash-8

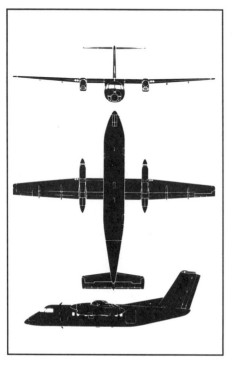

Nation: Canada

Versions: Series 100; Series 300 and 400 (stretched fuselage)

First flown: 1983

Length: 73.1ft (22.3m)   **Wingspan:** 85.0ft (25.9m)

Passenger capacity: 36-56

Cruising speed: 346mi (554km)/hr

Range: 1249mi (1998km)

Look-alikes: Dash-8 lacks the landing gear pods protruding from the lower part of the fuselage under the wings, present on *Avions de Transport Régional ATR 42/ATR 72.* In comparison to *Dash-8,* ATR 42/ATR 72 also have a differently shaped tailfin and a fuselage which extends further behind the tailfin.

A scaled down version of de Havilland's Dash-7, the Dash-8 is intended for commuter airline use. It has also been adapted by the military for use in versions including the Canadian Air Force CC-142 (passenger/cargo) and U.S. Air Force E-9A (surveillance/communications). *Specs:* Series 100; *Silhouette:* Series 100; *Side view silhouette:* Series 300; *Photo:* Series 100.

Photo courtesy Tony Honeywood/de Havilland Inc. Boeing Canada

Shorts 330

Nation: United Kingdom

Versions: 330-200 (passenger), 330-UTT (military transport), Sherpa (freighter with rear door)

First flown: 1974

Length: 58.1ft (17.7m)   **Wingspan:** 74.8ft (22.8m)

Passenger capacity: 30

Cruising speed: 220mi (352km)/hr

Range: 1059mi (1695km)

Look-alikes: The extended fuselage of Shorts 330 makes it easily distinguishable from the shorter fuselage of *Shorts Skyvan.*

The Shorts 330, an evolution of the Shorts Skyvan, was intended as an inexpensive 30 seat commuter transport. Over 100 have been sold. The plane is in service with the U.S. Air Force in its Sherpa freighter version as the C-23A.

Photo courtesy Short Brothers

Two props with wings high on fuselage

Shorts Skyvan

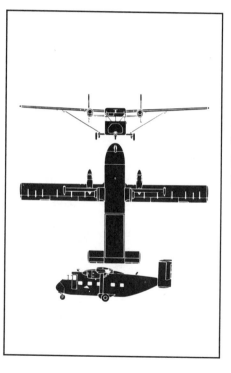

Nation: United Kingdom

Versions: Skyvan, Skyvan Series 2 and Series 3 (updated engines)

First flown: 1963

Length: 40.0ft (12.2m)   **Wingspan:** 64.9ft (19.8m)

Passenger capacity: 19

Freight capacity: 4641lb (2100kg)

Cruising speed: 200mi (320km)/hr

Range: 694mi (1110km)

Look-alikes: The foreshortened fuselage of Shorts Skyvan makes it easily distinguishable from the longer fuselage of *Shorts 360.*

The Skyvan was designed as a light freighter, and has been adapted to commuter passenger transport. In its freighter configuration, cargo is loaded through an underside rear door. The Shorts 330 is an enlarged version of the Skyvan. *Silhouette:* Series 3; *Photo:* Series 3.

Photo courtesy Short Brothers